Other giftbooks in this series:

Cat Quotations   Horse Quotations

Cricket Quotations   Golf Quotations

Published simultaneously in 1996 by Exley Publications in Great Britain and
Exley Giftbooks in the USA.

Copyright © Helen Exley 1996

12 11 10 9 8 7 6 5 4 3 2 1

ISBN 1-85015-775-8

A copy of the CIP data is available from the British Library on request. All
rights reserved. No part of this publication may be reproduced or transmitted
in any form or by any means, electronic or mechanical, including photocopy,
recording or any information storage and retrieval system without
permission in writing from the publisher.

Series Editor: Helen Exley.
Pictures selected by Helen Exley.
Words edited by Claire Lipscomb.
Pictures researched by Image Select, London.
With thanks to Margaret Montgomery for help with text research.
Designed by Pinpoint Design Company.
Typeset by Delta, Watford.
Printed and bound in Hungary.

Exley Publications Ltd, 16 Chalk Hill, Watford, Herts WD1 4BN, UK.
Exley Giftbooks, 232 Madison Avenue, Suite 1206, NY 10016, USA.

Acknowledgements: The publishers are grateful for permission to reproduce copyright
material. Whilst every effort has been made to trace copyright holders, we would be pleased to
hear from any not here acknowledged. SUE BARKER: Extracts from *Playing Tennis* © 1979 Sue
Barker. Reprinted by permission of B. T. Batsford Ltd. ELLIOT CHAZE: Extracts from "How
Tennis Has Changed" in *It Only Hurts When I Serve* ed. David Wiltse. Reprinted by permission
of Simon & Schuster, Inc. RICHARD EVANS: Extracts from *McEnroe/A Rage for Perfection: A
Biography* © 1982 Richard Evans. Reprinted by permission of MacMillan Publishers Ltd.
YANNICK NOAH: Extracts from *Tennis* © 1988 Yannick Noah. Reprinted by permission of
Editions Denoël, Paris. THEODOR SARETSKY: Extracts from *Sex as a Sublimation for Tennis
from The Secret Writings of Freud* © 1985 Theodor Saretsky. Reprinted by permission of
Workman Publishing Co. MONICA SELES: Extracts from *Monica from Fear to Victory* by
Monica Seles with Nancy Ann Richardson. Reprinted by permission of
HarperCollins*Publishers.* VIRGINIA WADE: Extracts from *Courting Triumph* by Virginia Wade
with Mary Lou Mellace © 1978 by Marksman International. Published by Hodder &
Stoughton. **Picture credits:** Exley Publications is very grateful to the following individuals and
organizations for permission to reproduce their pictures: Archiv für Kunst (AKG), The
Bridgeman Art Library (BAL), Edimedia (EDM), E.T. Archive (ET), Fine Art Photographic
Library (FAP), Giraudon (GIR), Mary Evans Picture Library (MEPL), Sotheby's Transparency
Library (STL), The Image Bank (TIB), Visual Arts Library (VAL): Cover: © 1996 Sir John
Lavery, *The Tennis Party*, BAL; title page: © 1996 Norman Merritt, TIB; p6: © 1996 Adolf
Münzer, MEPL; p9: MEPL; p10/11: © 1996 Charles March Gere, BAL; p12: Ferd von Reznicek,
MEPL; p14/15: © 1996 Valentine-Daines, VAL; p17: MEPL; p18: © 1996 Alexander Stuart
Boyd, VAL; p20/21: Spencer Gore, BAL; p22: © 1996 Scott Snow, TIB; p24: © 1996 Helen
Wills, VAL; p26: AKG; p28/9: © 1996 Lawrence Toynbee, VAL; p31: AKG; p32: © 1996 A.
Vallée, MEPL; p35: © 1996 Percy Shakespeare, FAP; p36: AKG; p39: MEPL; p40/41: G.D.
Rowlandson, AKG; p43: ET; p45: STL; p46: Alphonse Vermeylen, STL; p48/9: Gabrielle Bella,
GIR/BAL; p50: EDM; p53: © 1996 Robert Peak, TIB; p55: © 1996 Cecil Higgs, VAL; p56:
Theodore Lane, BAL; p58: © 1996 Sir John Lavery, FAP; p60: © 1996 Paul Ordner, MEPL.

TENNIS
QUOTATIONS

A COLLECTION OF APPEALING PICTURES AND THE BEST TENNIS QUOTES

EXLEY
NEW YORK • WATFORD, UK

TENNIS:
A SPORT FOR ALL

"Tennis has truthfully given me everything,
brought me everything: the people I've
met, travel, work, bad times, good
times, emotions....
I adore this sport: it's technical, physical and
mental, all at the same time.
Tennis is extraordinary because it is
played just about everywhere in the world
with the same enthusiasm, and by an
astonishing variety of individuals: from the
very young to the very old, the most clumsy
to the most talented...."

YANNICK NOAH

●

A WAY OF LIFE...

"Tennis has been the only constant thing in my life since I was a little girl and my parents found the money for me to join a club. I loved everything about it – the atmosphere, green grass, tea after matches and social life."

GLORIA HUNNIFORD

●

"I found myself immersed in tennis.... There was no experience that did not relate to tennis, no conversation that did not come back to tennis. Tennis was used as a parable for life. If something went wrong, there was a tennis lesson to be found in the occurrence. Tennis and life were one and the same."

LORI McNEIL

●

"The scene should be laid on a
well-kept garden lawn. There should be a
bright warm sun overhead, and
just sufficient breeze whispering through
the trees and stirring the petals of
the flowers to prevent the day from being
sultry. Near at hand, under the

cool shadow of a tree, there should be
strawberries and cream, iced claret mug, and
a few spectators who do not want to play, but
are lovers of a game, intelligent and
appreciative...."

LIEUTENANT-COLONEL R.D. OSBORN
from "Lawn Tennis – Its Players and How to Play"

AN OBSESSION

"In tennis the addict moves about a hard
rectangle and seeks to ambush a fuzzy ball
with a modified snow-shoe."

ELLIOT CHAZE
from "Strange How Tennis Has Changed"
in "It Only Hurts When I Serve"

"Why has slamming a ball with a racquet become so obsessive a pleasure for so many of us? It seems clear to me that a primary attraction of the sport is the opportunity it gives to release aggression physically without being arrested for felonious assault."

NAT HENTOFF
from "Murderous Pleasures of the Game"
in "It Only Hurts When I Serve"

●

"Just what is it about tennis that keeps me here? Isn't there something crazy about decking out in a little white costume made specially for me... to go racing back and forth on 1,000 or so square feet of turf, hitting a furry ball over a net in the middle? Why do grown people do this? Why was *I* doing this? If it wasn't crazy, what was it?"

VIRGINIA WADE

●

"I arrived late, in the orthodox costume
– that is to say, a straw hat
which is oftener off than on, a
flannel shirt two sizes too large
for me, and a pair of flannels...."

F. B. DOVETON
(At a Lawn Tennis Party)
from "A Fisherman's Fancies"

"The primary conception of tennis is to get the ball over the net and at the same time to keep it within bounds of the court; failing this, within the borders of the neighborhood."

ELLIOT CHAZE
from "Strange How Tennis Has Changed"
in "It Only Hurts When I Serve"

●

"'But how do you learn?'
'The way a tennis player learns to play tennis, by making a fool of yourself, by falling on your face, by rushing the net and missing the ball, and finally by practice....'"

MAY SARTON

●

"Good shot, bad luck and hell are the five basic words to be used in tennis."

VIRGINIA GRAHAM

●

Novice at
the game.

"I think about that sometimes – learning to play in a parking lot: stringing nets between cars.... I learned to play by hitting against a brick wall, not a ball machine or other players. And my father was my coach – teaching me from a twenty-year-old book, and a new system he developed. I was lucky my dad was so creative and capable. When I hear people say that you can't make it in tennis if you don't have a lot of money, I know they're wrong.... we didn't have much money. But I loved the sport, and that was enough."

MONICA SELES

●

"The child who enjoys playing tennis may be alone and, to a certain extent, this can be seen as either selfish or brave, but the child has to learn to win and lose gracefully, alone. This is a character building experience."

LISA SCULLY-O'GRADY

"Here was a game that would finally make real demands on my boundless energy. I got to run *and* hit a ball besides. I loved the quick and visible results when the ball and racquet connected and I was tantalised by the idea that there was something very exact about it."

VIRGINIA WADE

"Speed in tennis is a strange mixture of intuition, guesswork, footwork and hair-trigger reflexes. Many of the players famed for quickness on court would finish dead last in a field of schoolgirls in a race over any distance more than ten yards."

EUGENE SCOTT

ONE-ON-ONE

"Personally, I have always considered tennis
as a combat in an arena between two
gladiators who have their racquets and their
courage as their weapons."

YANNICK NOAH

●

"People think this is all about the top players
hitting tennis balls and they talk about
technique and strategy and how important
that is. But they don't understand the essence
of competition. This is one-on-one,
two players out there fighting each other
with everything they have, trying to bring the
best out of themselves. And the difference
at this level of the game is all in the head and
in the heart."

JOHN NEWCOMBE

●

"Tennis is a battle of minds, just as much as it is a battle of playing ability. Trying to expose your opponent's weakness is one of the most vital and fascinating facets of tennis."

SUE BARKER
from "Playing Tennis"

●

"Why is it that one minute you'd rather die than lose the point and another you literally give it away? Will power. Why does it come and go? I've practised tennis for twenty-two years; I've thought about the game for almost as long and then for a couple of minutes I allow a lapse of will and make enough silly errors to lose a game. It's ridiculous."

VIRGINIA WADE

●

"Don't relax your mind any more than you would relax your body. The penalty is the same – defeat."

SUE BARKER
from "Playing Tennis"

"I don't know why, but I love the dog-eat-dog nature of tennis. It's real, it's brutal and there's no hiding place, it's like a one-to-one street fight. I love the intensity that comes with knowing you walk off court either a winner or a loser. It's daunting but very exciting. There is no one to blame except yourself, no one cares who comes second."

PETE SAMPRAS

"... there is no such thing as a draw or even a tie in tennis. It is a fight to the death; no prisoners are taken and time is irrelevant. A tennis player can lead 6-0, 6-0, 5-0, 40-love and still end up a loser if he lacks the nerve to go through with the dirty business of winning; if he does not possess the matador's courage to go in over the horns for the kill."

RICHARD EVANS
from "McEnroe, A Rage for Perfection"

●

"I was always a believer in stamping on my opponent if I got him down, at Wimbledon or anywhere else. I never wanted to give him the chance to get up."

FRED PERRY

●

AN ESCAPE...

"Playing a good tennis match
gives you an overwhelming feeling of
elation. Nothing else in the world matters
at that point in time. All the
stress and strain of the mundane, the

housework, the nine-to-five job, are
buried and forgotten as you concentrate
on the game at hand."

LISA SCULLY-O'GRADY

DOUBLE TROUBLE!

"I suppose, as Frew says, it's a
bit like a marriage really. You cherish your
partner, help them out in times of trouble
and look with confidence for assistance
when you're in a spot of bother yourself. It's
certainly true that nobody ever won a doubles
match by himself or herself."

SUE BARKER
from "Playing Tennis"

●

"The tide was out today for us during our
game of tennis... a dodgy forehand, weak
backhand or rather my second shot just
wasn't there! There's always a good excuse for
a lost doubles match."

LISA SCULLY-O'GRADY

●

"An otherwise happily married couple may turn a mixed doubles game into a scene from *Who's afraid of Virginia Woolf.*"

ROD LAVER

"What a polite game tennis is. The chief word in it seems to be 'sorry' and admiration of each other's play crosses the net as frequently as the ball."

J. M. BARRIE

"Sometimes, a defeat can be more beautiful and satisfying than certain victories. The English have a point in insisting that it matters not who won or lost, but how you played the game."

ARTHUR ASHE
from "Days of Grace"

●

"It's about good long rallies and fun, not about thrashing your opponent."

LISA SCULLY-O'GRADY

●

"After a desperate fight, to know to congratulate your opponent, if he has beaten you, to shake his hand and go for a drink with him, in my eyes these things are particularly important."

YANNICK NOAH

●

QUIET PLEASE...

"Different crowds have different cheering routines. In Germany and Scandinavia, they like to stomp their feet. At the Guayaquil Tennis Club stadium in Ecuador, there was always a group way up in the tops of the stands under the Coca-Cola sign that would ring a cowbell. The umpire would call for silence, but it didn't do any good. The fans would quiet down when they felt like it."

ARTHUR ASHE
from "Arthur Ashe on Tennis"

●

"The Centre Court at Wimbledon is an intimidating arena; it is, in a sense, a cathedral of the game and even the noisiest and most extrovert personalities tend to be dwarfed by its all-embracing atmosphere."

RICHARD EVANS
from "Open Tennis"

●

"I prefer to stay at home and watch it [Wimbledon] on the telly – from the comfort of an armchair that I can hide behind if things get too exciting."

CHRISTOPHER BIGGINS, British actor,
from "OK!", July 7, 1996

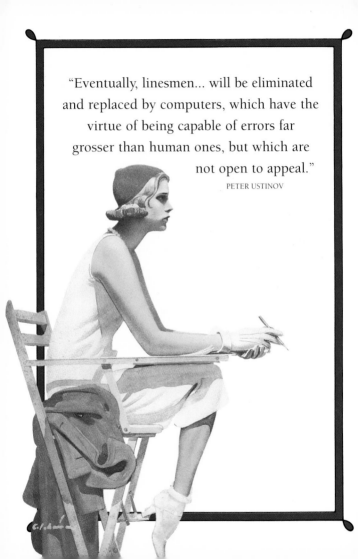

"Eventually, linesmen... will be eliminated and replaced by computers, which have the virtue of being capable of errors far grosser than human ones, but which are not open to appeal."

PETER USTINOV

"In the game of tennis a player calls shots in or out and, according to the rules and etiquette of the game, may have absolute jurisdiction. Since personal integrity is involved, most players reconcile this with their underlying competitive cutthroat instincts by becoming unconscious liars. Concrete evidence for this distortion of reality is hard to come by; however, present in the history of most individuals who make bad calls is the widely known nursery rhyme 'When in Doubt, Call It Out'."

THEODOR SARETSKY

●

"I excused myself by expressing myself flattered by the offer, but begged them to renew it when my eyesight had deteriorated sufficiently for me to be able to make wrong decisions with absolute conviction."

PETER USTINOV
on being asked to be a linesman at Wimbledon

"Tennis is not a gentle game.
Psychologically, it is vicious. That people are
only just beginning to come to terms with
this fact illustrates just how big a con trick
has been perpetrated on the non-playing
tennis public – and even a few players,
usually losing players – for decades."

RICHARD EVANS
from "McEnroe, A Rage for Perfection"

●

"Winning is about taking your opponent's
heart out and squeezing it until all the blood
has come out, even the very last drop. There
are no prizes for a funny loser."

PETE SAMPRAS

●

"Whoever said, 'It's not whether you win or
lose that counts', probably lost."

MARTINA NAVRATILOVA

●

"Tennis is a perfect combination of violent action taking place in an atmosphere of tranquility."

BILLIE JEAN KING

<u>TEMPER, TEMPER!</u>

"The cunning competitor plays on the other party's guilt. Continuously praise your opponent's shots, and you'll notice how he begins to press. Self-beratement also serves to balance a guilty conscience for being successful and makes your opponent disturbed for upsetting you so. If on occasion you call one of your opponent's 'out' shots 'in', then later on you can innocently call an 'in' shot 'out' on a crucial play. Practice saying 'Good try,' sincerely; then you can call a lot of close shots 'out' and get away with it."

THEODOR SARETSKY

●

"You are the pits of the world!
Vultures! Trash!"

JOHN McENROE
to the umpire, spectators and reporters at Wimbledon,
quoted in "*Time*", December 28, 1981

●

"Nastase rarely grins and bears it. More commonly he grins, groans, shrugs, slumps, spins around, shakes his head, puffs out his cheeks, rolls on the ground and bears it. Even more common, he does all that and doesn't bear it."

CLIVE JAMES

●

"I don't know that my behavior has improved that much with age. They just found somebody worse."

JIMMY CONNERS

●

DOWN WITH TENNIS!

"Tennis... is too violent a motion for wholesome exercise, for those that play much at tennis impair their health and strength by wasting their vital spirits through much sweating, and weaken their nerves by overstraining them. Neither can tennis be a pastime, which is only a recreation, and there can be no recreation in sweaty labour."

MARGARET CAVENDISH, DUCHESS OF NEWCASTLE

●

"A vain, idle and sinful game at which there was much of the language of the accursed going on."

JAMES HOGG,
Scottish poet

●

THE ART OF TENNIS

"It's difficult for most people to imagine the creative process in tennis. Seemingly it's just an athletic matter of hitting the ball consistently well within the boundaries of the court. That analysis is just as specious as thinking that the difficulty in portraying King Lear on stage is learning all the lines."

VIRGINIA WADE

●

"Tennis is like a game of chess, with limitless different approaches."

VIRGINIA WADE

●

"It takes far more than just hitting a ball to be the very best and to reach your own highest point, not only in sports but in life."

NICK BOLLETTIERI

●

"More than anything, winning the Grand Slam is a battle within yourself. It really gets down to how you handle pressure more than how you handle anybody else."

MARGARET COURT

"Sport strips away personality, letting the white bone of character shine through. Sport gives players an opportunity to know and test themselves."

RITA MAE BROWN
from "Sudden Death"

Gioco Della Racchetta

"There's nothing quite as therapeutic as a nice new dress to make you feel ready for the fray. Clothes do wonders for your ego, especially on the Centre Court."

VIRGINIA WADE

"The first dress she wore at Wimbledon came just below her knee, and the sleeves barely reached past her elbows. Up until then women had been wearing ankle-length skirts, blouses with corsets, and long sleeves. The dress created almost as much controversy as Suzanne did by drinking cognac during the changeovers."

MONICA SELES
on Suzanne Lenglen

"I didn't want to cause anybody to spill their strawberries and cream."

ANNE WHITE,
US tennis player, on her appearance at Wimbledon
in a white alabaster body stocking

"... like boxing, there is nowhere for a tennis player to hide; no chance of skiving off to long leg for a breather, nor even the momentary respite for a batsman of being at the non-striker's end.... With tennis the spotlight is unceasing and unmerciful. Often for as long as four hours – not far short of *three* times the length of a soccer match – a tennis player must keep body and mind tuned to the highest pitch of concentration and competitive drive in a sport that demands control and precision as well as gut-wrenching bursts of speed and power. Anyone for tennis?"

RICHARD EVANS
from "McEnroe, A Rage for Perfection"

●

"People don't seem to understand that it's a damn war out there."

JIMMY CONNERS

●

"You know, when you lose like that, you are like naked in front of the whole world."

ILIE NASTASE

●

"I have seriously thought about retiring, but that was on a good day. On a bad day I've thought about killing myself."

IVAN LENDL

●

"Losing still hurts, but that's good. When it stops hurting, that's when I stop playing."

MARTINA NAVRATILOVA

●

"The great champions don't hide when they lose; they go out on the practice court and pledge never to let it happen again."

JOHN LLOYD

●

"I haven't lost a war. No one got killed. I just lost a tennis match."

BORIS BECKER,
commenting on his second round defeat at Wimbledon,
as defending champion, in 1987

"Remember the glow you used to get when your service came around, the fresh steel of forearm, shoulder and calf? You didn't even have to think about it. You pondered your suntan, your date for the evening and the achingly beautiful prospect of Swiss steak and butter beans for supper.

Sometimes you barely realized you'd served until the ball hissed over the taped rim of the net.

That's all different now, I find.

When I cranked up, there was a bleak crunch in the working shoulder, the sort of thing one hears when cutting a deck of lettuce with the edge of a fork."

ELLIOT CHAZE
from "Strange How Tennis Has Changed"
in "It Only Hurts When I Serve"

LIFE AFTER TENNIS...

"If you can react the same way to winning and losing, that's a big accomplishment. That quality is important because it stays with you the rest of your life, and there's going to be a life after tennis that's a lot longer than your tennis life."

CHRIS EVERT-LLOYD

●

"I'm looking forward to it very much. I think it beats the hell out of life after death, that's for sure."

MARTINA NAVRATILOVA

●

"When I was forty, my doctor advised me that a man in his forties shouldn't play tennis. I heeded his advice carefully and could hardly wait until I reached fifty to start again."

JUSTICE HUGO BLACK

●

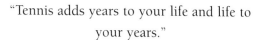

"Tennis adds years to your life and life to
your years."

ROY WILDER

"The only possible regret I have
is the feeling that I will die without
having played enough tennis."

JEAN BOROTRA

●

"Ask Nureyev to stop dancing, ask Sinatra
to stop singing – then you can ask me to
stop playing tennis."

BILLIE JEAN KING

●

"We all aspire to win the Grand Slams of our
unique lives. Although our victories seem to
be isolated acts, perhaps they are the gift we
are given when we remain faithful to
the process, the long, laborious
process of conquering our most formidable
opponent, ourselves."

LORI McNEIL

●